THE NEW BUSINESS IDEAS

21 SIMPLE BUSINESS MODELS TO BUILD **YOUR** OWN STARTUP

- By James Willner -

Copyright © 2018 James Willner
All rights reserved.

ISBN-13: 978-1725136533
ISBN-10: 1725136538

The following eBook is reproduced below with the goal of providing information that is as accurate and as reliable as possible. Regardless, purchasing this eBook be consent to the fact that both the publisher and the author of this book are in no way experts on the topics discussed within, and that any recommendations or suggestions made herein are for entertainment purposes only. Professionals should be consulted as needed before undertaking any of the action endorsed herein.

This declaration is deemed fair and valid by both the American Bar Association and the Committee of Publishers Association and is legally binding throughout the United States.

Furthermore, the transmission, duplication or reproduction of any of the following work, including precise information, will be considered an illegal act, irrespective whether it is done electronically or in print. The legality extends to creating a secondary or tertiary copy of the work or a recorded copy and is only allowed with express written consent of the Publisher. All additional rights are reserved.

The information in the following pages is broadly considered to be a truthful and accurate account of facts, and as such any inattention, use, or misuse of the information in question by the reader will render any resulting actions solely under their purview. There are no scenarios in which the publisher or the original author of this work can be in any fashion deemed liable for any hardship or damages that may befall them after undertaking information described herein.

Additionally, the information found on the following pages is intended for informational purposes only and should thus be considered, universal. As befitting its nature, the information presented is without assurance regarding its continued validity or interim quality. Trademarks that mentioned are done without written consent and can in no way be considered an endorsement from the trademark holder.

Table of contents

Introduction 5
Why You Should Start Your Own Business ? 8
Droning Service 17
Event Planning 22
Delivery Services 28
Independent Marketing Consultant 34
Pet Services 39
Travel Planner 45
Photography and Videography 49
e-Commerce Store 56
Patient Advocate 64
Freelance Content Creator 68
Website Buyer and Flipper 76
Graphic Designer 81
Online Dating Consultant 85
Affiliate Marketer 88
Social Media Manager 92
Blogging 97
Chatbot Creator 102
Craft Brewery 105
Crafter 108
Tour Guide 116
Repair Services 120
Conclusion 127

THE NEW BUSINESS IDEAS

INTRODUCTION

Welcome and thank you for joining in on *The NEW Business Ideas.*

Let's face it; most 9 to 5 jobs *suck*. You must report to your job at a certain time, trapped there for 8 hours, are not promised breaks, and have to follow the orders of a demeaning boss. But this is what you spent a fortune on, to get educated and fall into the 9 to 5 "norm," right?

What if I told you that there are thousands of other people that have broken free from the 9 to 5 shackles? They get to create a schedule that best suits *them* and are excited to wake up because they enjoy what they do, all from the comforts of their own home?

Sounds *way* too good to be true? Trust me, I thought of the same thing! That is until I stumbled across the power that the ever-changing world wide web had to offer.

While you're reading this in 2018, the advancements of the internet are continuous, creating more opportunities to make a part or full-time income from the online world.

How would your life change if:

- You could spend more time with your family?
- If you could make an additional income to help pay off debt?
- If you could create your own schedule and travel whenever you pleased?
- Did not have to report to that terrible boss of yours?
- Never had to wait in traffic again?

The world of a better-suited income is not only confined to the means of the internet either! There are plenty of easy-to-implement business ideas you can start, develop, and build from the

THE NEW BUSINESS IDEAS

comforts of your own home! But the additional power of the internet sure doesn't hurt!

The following chapters will discuss 21 creative business ideas that you can learn more about. There is a strong possibility that you will find your future place of employment at your own home office!

Everyone deserves to build a life of financial freedom and gain their time back from working for companies that don't see their best interest. In this book, I hope you find a new business model that you can start to build yourself, as soon as *today*.

Every effort was made to ensure it is full of as much useful information as possible, please enjoy!

WHY YOU SHOULD START YOUR OWN BUSINESS ?

"Starting a business is risky."
"You will go straight into a pool of debt!"
"Be prepared to not get a good night's sleep for a while."
"You are going to bail on your social life?"

The list goes on and on when it comes to the 'reasons' people have when you tell them that you are interested in starting your own business. I am sure you have heard a great spiel of them. Those reasons, however, are just excuses.

If you are still attracted to the world of entrepreneurship, then you may have what it takes to develop your own business that you can run on *your* terms.

However, if the reasons above make you a bit on edge, then let's talk about the many more reasons that you *should* take the leap and start your own business!

Change the world

It can be hard to imagine how a cell phone kiosk at the mall can have the power to change the world, but there are many of these places that do succeed. Look at Bill Gates and many of the other infamous entrepreneurs who have changed our world in big and small ways! Everyone must start somewhere.

Reinvention

Every time entrepreneurs sell a company they have built, they are almost always presented with new opportunities to reinvent themselves.

Spare time

When you first start a business, you will work longer hours for less pay. However, if you do things properly, you can master your own schedule and develop the freedom that all successful entrepreneurs have!

A good story

When you tell people that you own a business, they are curious to know what you do, how you do it, and how things are going for you. This helps you to tell a tale of two and the best part? You are the author of your business's storybook!

Awesome tax benefits

For entrepreneurs and freelancers, there are many opportunities they have to take advantage of tax perks. There are many things they can write off, such as phone bill, food, travel, portions of payments for car(s) and their home, etc. There are also some startups that qualify to receive incentives from the government.

A sense of pride

When you are able to build something successful from the ground up, it is obviously a good feeling. This means you had a vision and you were able to execute it. Then, you reap the benefits from all your hard work.

Would you be prouder of building a business yourself or getting the millionth proposal required from your employer?

Posterity

There are some jobs, such as a bus driver, plumber, or doctor, that can be hard to imagine passing it down to loved ones. However, when you own your business, this is something that can easily be passed down for generations.

Job security

If you have ever been fired or laid-off from your job, it is a terrible feeling. This is why entrepreneurship is so great since there is a sense of security that lies within you being your own boss. You are the one that runs things, and you don't have to worry about being let go.

Networking

Entrepreneurs are naturally communal creatures. We love to meet new people, share stories, and learn from one another's experiences. As an entrepreneur, your circle of acquaintances and friends continues to grow since founders need others to lean on to talk about relatable challenges.

Spread goodness

This perk is not exclusive to entrepreneurs, but you have control over the company, which means you control where your profits go. You can sponsor others or donate to a charity. This is one of the most feel-good advantages to owning your own business once you get firmly on your feet.

Novelty

As human beings, we all enjoy new experiences. However, from inside a cubicle, we rarely get to experience new things. By running your own business, you can ensure that you will face brand-new, challenging and exciting experiences.

Mentorship

Getting to mentor others after you have had the failures and successes of building a business is very rewarding. Learning from the experts gives beginners a sense of satisfaction in their everyday lives. It is good to give back and lend a helping hand to those trying to change their lives with a startup.

Becoming an expert

No matter what you do as an entrepreneur, if you stick with it for the long haul, you will become great at it. This then gives you a soapbox that you can use. You will have a better chance to be seen and asked questions by others about your expertise, which gives you the chance to write and spread the word about your experiences.

Gain skills

Developing new skills is not the easiest, but they can add invaluable assets to your life and business. Through my freelance business, I learned how to do SEO (search engine optimization), social media, and other marketing techniques. I was also forced to learn how to use spreadsheets, balance budgets, and negotiate with others.

Determination

The things you do as an entrepreneur will affect you positively in your everyday life. I used to be terrible at committing to change. But now as a freelancer, I have been forced to become dedicated and determined to my cause. My business seeps into my personal life by making me more dedicated to things such as eating healthy and exercising regularly, for instance.

Recognition

There are thousands of various awards that vary from local, regional, to national that are made to recognize entrepreneurs in a variety of fields. This should not be your only or first reason to start a business. However, it is a great feeling to be recognized for all your hard work.

Financial independence

This is probably the most common reason people take the leap to develop a business of their very own. Financial independence allows you to add to your retirement, gives you unlimited cash potential, which then gives you the freedom to travel and do whatever you wish to do. Entrepreneurship is one of the best paths to achieve this kind of freedom. However, money does not buy happiness, but it sure does make finding happiness easier.

Now, on to the good stuff!

I am sure you have read several perks that peaked your interest in learning more about starting a business of your own. Now, let's get into the meat of the book and discuss the **21** business ideas for all walks of life!

THE NEW BUSINESS IDEAS

DRONING SERVICE

There has never been a better time to start droning. With the advancements in drone technology, the average Joe can now buy quality affordable drones that are simple to learn and use. This means it is not only easy to fly but an easy money-maker.

Beginner Steps to Starting a Drone Business

Make a small investment

If you want to fly drones for more than just a fun weekend hobby, the Federal Aviation Administration (FAA) requires pilots to receive a Remote Pilot Airman Certificate.

Also, if you have a drone that is over 0.55 pounds, you will need to register it with the FAA as well. The best practice if you wish to make money droning is to comply with FAA regulations.

Average start-up costs are $150, plus a $5 registration for each drone you own and register.

Start shooting

Get to know your drone *well*. Learn what you drone is built for. Some drones are stable and high-quality for filming, while others are durable and speedy for racing. There are also survey drones that are built to carry specialized equipment.

The more you practice and learn about your drone, the better. Make interesting videos and take photos from cool angles. This can help you gain recognition! There are drone film festivals that you can compete at, but be prepared to go against drone pros. There are also drone websites that let you set up donations that can later get you hired for filming assignment.

Fly commercially

There are hundreds of ways that drones can provide services that can make you quite a chunk of change. From Amazon delivery to scanning farms, there are needs for commercial drones in many fields.

Many industrial companies are hiring drone pilots and pay between $50,000 to $70,000, depending on your expertise and the type of drone you are flying. However, this is the pay likely for those that used to be helicopter pilots, not novice flyers.

If you engage in weekend drone gigs or contract work, you can still expect to make upwards of $2,000 to $7,000+ per job, depending on your role. You can look for drone jobs on specialized job boards, such as Dronebase.com. There are also industries such as real estate that will post on their site for pilots.

Drone Business Ideas

Photography and videography

This drone service is the most popular service that is now affordable for just about everyone to get starting. Images and video taken from a birds-eye perspective cannot be matched to what is taken from the ground.

- Landscape
- Sports
- Real estate
- Wildlife
- Weddings
- Film and television
- Special events

Security surveillance

Security for home and commercial locations is another droning opportunity. If there are trespassers, drones can notify the right people when activated. They can detect threats to property and send live feeds to property owners.

Search and rescue

Drones are becoming a popular tool in search and rescue missions around the globe. It greatly reduces the cost of helicopters and drones are able to fly at night into places where helicopters cannot go. Becoming an operator can be a great and rewarding business opportunity!

Other Drone Business Ideas:

- Building inspections
- Agricultural surveys
- Drone sales
- Drone training
- Drone customization
- Insurance inspections
- Drone regulations
- Drone insurance

James Willner

EVENT PLANNING

Many event planners start their business from home, which makes it a great business model if you are looking to keep overhead costs down while trading your services and maximizing your profits.

Working events and meetings outside of the office setting can be a great profession to pursue, especially if you already have experience in these environments.

Steps to Start an Event Planning Business

Gain event planning skills

If you want long-term success, it will depend on what you are bringing to your potential clients. This means you need a solid understanding of what event planners do and what they need to know. You will need:

- Verbal and written communication skills
- Organization and time management skills
- Budget management
- Negotiation skills
- Creativity
- Marketing
- Public relations

Decide on your market

Common mistake event planners make when creating their business is telling themselves that they are equipped with the expertise to coordinate all types of events, from corporate to wedding and more.

While it is great to offer a wide array of services to clients, but you need to recognize that there are distinct differences between events. Start out in one market and work your way up.

Create a business plan

Before you share the news of the business you are developing, you need to develop a solid business plan. My personal favorite resource is heading over to the U.S. Small Business Administration website where you can find materials about business plans.

Designate a business entity

Now you need to decide what business structure you want. Ensure that the type of entity you choose suits your business plan. It is a good idea to get some professional advice.

Get business insurance

Business insurance is a must. You should secure at least a general liability to protect your business. There are many types of insurance so you may need to speak with an insurance advisor to decide what is best for you.
- General liability
- Product liability

- Home-based insurance
- Worker's compensation
- Criminal insurance
- Health

Create a network of suppliers and staffing resources

You will need to lighten the burden of your business at some point, which you can do with a solid network of suppliers, such as photographers, florists, caterers, and more.

You may think you can handle all the tasks, but the bigger your business becomes, the more you are going to need an infrastructure established to support your events and operations accordingly.

Define your services

What kind of event services do you plan to offer through your business? Will you specialize in just one or several aspects of planning? Or will you provide full-service planning that includes venues, transportation, lodging, production, catering, speakers, and more?

Create a fee structure

It is important to determine a fee structure when you are running a service-oriented business. This will help the business thrive long-term.

- Flat fee
- Percentage of your expenses
- Hourly rate
- Percentage of expenses and hourly rate
- Commissionable rate

Secure funding

In all cases, you will not have to do this, but it is also vital to remain motivated by the work you will need to do in order to bring your new business to life. This is why a source of funding is a good idea. You will need some sort of operating budget so that you can access it.

It is more than possible to establish a business with limited funds, but you will need enough funds to start your business while covering living expenses while you wait for your business to turn a profit.

Focus on development and marketing

Now that your business model is in place and you understand your services and what you plan to charge, now you will need to develop your business with the help of marketing.

Choose a good name for your business and work on your business plan continuously. Create business cards, a website, proposals, agreements, and more.

James Willner

DELIVERY SERVICES

If you are a sociable individual who enjoys meeting and conversing with new people, then a delivery service is right up your alley.

Delivery service is a business that anyone has the capability to start. It can be offered in hundreds of niches and can vary from running personal errands for people to delivering packages for big box companies. This is a great option if you want to be your own boss and make a decent living without too much hassle and pesky overhead.

Steps to Start Delivering

Get a vehicle

Depending on what you are delivering, you will likely need a truck or van to haul items. There is a huge market for used vehicles. Cargo vans, trucks, and pickups are your best bet for a delivery business. If you plan to deliver food and similar items, consider a smaller, more fuel-efficient choice.

Gather equipment

Once you have your vehicle, you will need to determine the equipment you need to ensure smooth deliveries.

- Dolly
- Straps
- Tarps
- Red flags

Pick a name

Business names are vital to your success. Be creative! Once you have a good, unique name that stands out from the crowd, you can go to websites like LegalZoom.com to find resources to ensure your business is legal. Speak with an accountant and a lawyer to determine if you should keep your business a sole proprietorship or an LLC.

Market your business

Successful business means you need consumers!

- Tell your family and friends about your business
- Post of social media
- Create your own website
- Create business cards and flyers

Build a reputation

Once you start receiving delivery jobs, you need to ensure you execute excellent time and time again. If you are consistent, you'll most likely get a good reputation. Provide great customer service and communicate well with consumers and those helping you out, if there are any.

Insurance

As a business owner, you should always consider what kind of insurance is best to protect you and your livelihood in case an accident occurs. You come off as much more reliable when you have your delivery company insured. Remember that the costs and types of insurance will be based on where you are located, the kinds of deliveries you are making, and the risk perceived.

- Car insurance
- Liability insurance

Keep receipts

Tracking expenses is a very essential part of being a small business owner. Expenses that are related to your business can help you save lots of money during tax season as write-offs. I suggest using an app such as Expensify that is useful in tracking your expenses and receipts.

Types of Delivery Services:

- Legal notice delivery
- Print delivery
- Machinery hauler
- Grocery delivery
- Egg delivery
- Furniture delivery/assembly

- Sandwich/salad delivery
- Bread/milk delivery
- Computer delivery/assembly
- Online ordering
- Coffee delivery
- Clothing subscription
- Eyeglass delivery
- Fruit delivery
- Bottled water delivery
- Pizza delivery
- Transplant organ courier
- Laboratory test delivery
- Pet food delivery
- Community delivery
- Auto parts delivery
- Balloon delivery
- Office supply delivery
- Liquor delivery
- Air freight delivery
- School supply delivery
- Flyer delivery
- School bus services

THE NEW BUSINESS IDEAS

- Restaurant delivery
- Bicycle service
- After hours delivery
- Rental table/chair delivery
- Medical supply delivery
- Dinner ingredient delivery
- Drug delivery
- Dry cleaning delivery
- Diaper delivery
- Senior errand service
- Flower delivery
- Quick messenger
- Mail order delivery
- Lunch delivery
- Gift basket delivery
- Courier service

James Willner

INDEPENDENT MARKETING CONSULTANT

If you enjoy the art of marketing and the concept of finding creative ways to connect to the public the products and services they can benefit from, then developing your own independent marketing consultant company may be for you! You can work independently or perform contract work with marketing firms.

What is a marketing consultant?

These folks are professionals that work side by side with businesses to identify their needs when it comes to marketing their products and/or services. They create effective plans to promote their businesses. Many people enjoy this choice of career since it allows them to work with freedom with a variety of businesses.

Knowledge needed

- Some marketing education or experience
- Knowledgeable of social media platforms
- Search engine optimization (SEO) know-how
- Reputation management
- Image creation
- Basic technical know-how

Setting Up a shop

Before you start your search for clients that could benefit from your consulting services, you will need to ensure you have a workspace that breeds success. Here is a thorough checklist of the essential parts of your home office you will need:

Designated work area

Even if you don't have a separate office or a room to create one in, you still need a designated area to place your office that you can make strictly for work purposes.

Good office furniture

Luckily, quality office furniture doesn't have to be pricey. If you are developing your business on a tight budget, check into second-hand stores. You want furniture that you will find comfortable to sit at for long hours.

Computer and mobile device

You cannot expect to get ahead and stand out if you don't have access to the internet. Having a laptop, PC, and cellular device is a must if you are building any marketing business.

Ensure you have proper internet security and software to protect you and client's information from hackers.

Separate phone

You should not use your personal cell phone number as a business number. It is a good idea to secure a line that is dedicated to your clients and business so they can reach out if they have issues. Many freelancers enjoy the VoIP service, which is an affordable phone service through the internet.

Website, online resume, and portfolio

To impress and attract clients, they are going to check your work, and by that, you mean business. Before you start your client search, make sure you have a clean website created that houses your portfolio, resume, and other things about you as a marketing consultant.

Finding Clients

One of the most challenging ordeals as an independent business owner in any field is locating potential clients. When you work under another company, their brand has already been established. When you are on your own, however, it is up to you to create a brand for yourself. Here are some ways you can impress and attract paying clients:

- Create pages on social media platforms that will showcase your business
- Add your business signature to the bottom of your emails
- Participate in networking functions for small businesses
- Register yourself on freelance job sites and advertise/bid on contracts
- Gain letters of recommendation from past employers or clients
- Offer to intern on projects for free to show off your skills
- Check into job posting sites daily
- Follow and interact with people on relevant blogs

The ironic thing about this business model is that you must market yourself in order to build a client base. This is a great model because you literally are forced to practice marketing yourself and your business in order to get clients and gain long-term success.

THE NEW BUSINESS IDEAS

PET SERVICES

When it comes to our love of pets, all humans are alike! We would do anything and spend gobs of money to make our furry friends happy in our homes. This means that as an entrepreneur, there are *tons* of business opportunities you can start from home.

Yes, there are basic pet services such as training, grooming, walking, etc. But there are also many unique pet business ideas out there that you should seriously consider starting.

- **Organic treat maker**: Many pet owners are becoming more concerned with the ingredients in their pet's food and treats.
- **Obedience expert**: If you have the knowledge, you can carve out a unique niche in training, working with dogs on their habits.
- **Yard and in-home cleaning**: One of the biggest "pet" peeves for owners is having to

clean up after their pets, a market you can profit largely from.

- **Animal blogger**: You should start your own blog if you like sharing photos of pets and tips to make being a pet parent easier.

- **Animal toy creator**: Toys from big box stores can be *pricey,* which leaves you with the opportunity to create pet toys at cheap costs.

- **Travel service provider**: Travelling and moving with pets is stressful. You can offer a service that helps people transport their pets.

- **Pet bandana maker**: Simply pet bandanas are all the rage and can be sold online or at pet stores.

- **Cat café operator**: Coffee shops that allow customers to hang out with felines are becoming a big hit! Open one yourself.

- **Canine manicurist**: Just like groomers, you can make a nice chunk of change by trimming both dog's and cat's nails.

THE NEW BUSINESS IDEAS

- **Unique pet store operator**: Sure, there are tons of pet stores that sell things for average pets like dogs and cats, but what about the other guys? Open a pet store dedicated to exotic pets, such as birds and snakes.

- **Cat toilet trainer**: Cat owners would love if they no longer had to deal with their feline's stinky litter boxes.

- **Pet bakery owner**: Open a bakery that specializes specifically in pet food and treats.

- **Dog beer brewer**: There are many creative folks out there that have created a non-alcoholic beer for their pups. Enjoy brewing? Consider opening a brewery for dog beer.

- **YouTube training expert**: If you're an introvert and would rather train people about their pets without leaving your home, then start a YouTube channel dedicated to informing pet owners on various training methods.

- **Breath mint maker**: No one loves their pet's breath, especially when they are all up in your grill. Create pet breath mints!

- **Pet portraiture artist**: For those that love pets and have an artistic side, offer services to paint people's pets!

- **Pet photographer**: If you are not great with a paintbrush but better skilled with a camera, perhaps taking photos of people's pet is more of your style.

- **Pet clothing designer**: There are many owners that like dressing up their fur babies, even if their pets hate it. Design cute clothes for fur balls.

- **Luxury boarding operator**: When owners are away from home, it can be a pain to find a boarder or a sitter for their beloved furry family members. Offer a more luxurious boarding experience with spa services, real-time streaming, private rooms and more.

THE NEW BUSINESS IDEAS

- **At-home boarding**: For those that want their pets in the comfort of their own homes while they are away, provide people with an in-home boarding service.

- **Dog treat truck operator**: Instead of ice cream trucks for humans, start a treat truck for canines!

- **Homemade pet food creator**: Instead of people buying food from big box stores, they can buy your handmade goods.

- **Shelter matching expert**: There are so many ways that people search for potential pets. There are even at-home businesses that people have started where they create apps and websites to help match folks with their perfect pet!

- **Treat subscription service**: Another unique way to sell your homemade treats is to start a subscription box service.

- **Pet massage therapist**: Massages, just like for humans, are beneficial for cats, dogs, and many others of the animal kingdom. All you need is a bit of training to get started.

- **Pet health expert**: There are many concerned pet owners that turn to Google or spend thousands of dollars in vet bills each year when they think something is wrong with their pet. Offer basic tips to these folks.

- **Pet business marketing specialist**: Since there is such a vast array of business ideas in the pet niche, there are people out there that you can help to find their niche and market it correctly!

THE NEW BUSINESS IDEAS

TRAVEL PLANNER

Travel costs are always on the rise, which means people are looking for cheaper ways to secure deals and save money. If you have a knack for finding deals on rentals, hotels, and airline tickets, perhaps starting a business as a travel planner/agent is a good choice.

Starting a travel planning business from home is much easier than you may think, especially if you already own a computer and a phone. If you are a creative thinker, then you can even narrow down your business to specialize as a planner for travelers in a specific niche, such as romantic getaways or family vacations.

If you want a larger base for clients, then you can create different packages and custom deals for them and their needs. No matter what, clients who work with you will save money and will be better off financially while enjoying themselves!

Skills required

You will need to have fundamental computer knowledge to be a successful travel planner. You also need to familiarize yourself with travel and booking websites. Organization and time management skills are a must to run this sort of planning business. Clients will, of course, be expecting you to locate deals for them in a timely fashion.

Expenses to start – around $100

The startup costs to run a travel planning business are very low. If you already have a computer and phone, then you are practically ready! The biggest investment you will have to make is the advertising you will need to spread the word about your services. You can do this through the grapevine, online classifieds, posting on free boards, as well as social media.

Expected monthly revenue - $1,000 to $2,000+ per month

The time and energy you have to invest in your advertising will greatly impact how much money your work from home business will generate. When the word spreads about your online expertise, then your business will really begin to take off.

Expected monthly expenses - $100

The main monthly costs you will need to pay are for maintaining active advertising campaigns and the basic office supplies you will be using daily.

Amount of time you can expect to break even – 2 months

Within a two-month period, you should be able to attract the interest of enough people to recoup the startup costs for a travel planning business. This is a unique opportunity that allows you to make a nice chunk of additional cash while you are positively impacting people's lives and their wallets.

THE NEW BUSINESS IDEAS

PHOTOGRAPHY AND VIDEOGRAPHY

If you have a creative knack when it comes to shooting epic photos and/or videos, then you might have the talent to be successful with your very own photography and/or videography business.

While photography is a popular hobby and profession, this can pose a problem for beginners if they wish to stand out amongst the crowd. Thankfully, camera equipment has become more consumer friendly and affordable over the years, which means anyone can get what they need to become a photographer/videographer.

Planning Your Photography Business

Before you get yourself a camera and a website, you will need to follow these few steps to prepare:

Create a business plan

Any entrepreneur who is serious about a business venture knows the importance of creating an actionable business plan. This is a roadmap that breaks down your competition, ownership, expenses, cash flow, etc.

Since photography and videography is one of the most competitive businesses in the world, you need a rock-solid business plan to ensure you are starting off on the right foot.

Assess your financial needs for startup

You will need access to startup funds, which should be a portion of your business plan. Quality camera equipment alone can venture into tens of thousands of dollars. You will also need to get an accounting software, a website, insurance, and a business license.

Get startup funds

You may not need to borrow any money if you have quite a bit in savings, but many entrepreneurs need that extra assistance. You can ask family, friends, or apply for a bank loan.

Gain experience

In order to get clients, you will need to be able to show them your photography and videography capabilities. I highly suggest shadowing a professional photographer to gain insight and to expand your portfolio.

Purchase camera gear

As a beginner, you may not need two cameras, but once you continue to become more knowledgeable, you may want to look into getting another camera, which means you will need to double the equipment.

If you buy everything you need at once at a used price, it will be somewhere in the range of $5,000. If you buy everything new, expect to spend $10,000 or more. Plus, keep in mind you will likely upgrade your gear as the years go by in your business.

Develop a pricing plan

How much do you plan to charge clients for your services? Decide what is worth an hour of your time. Expect for each hour of shoot time that you will spend an additional three hours editing those photos. This will need to be factored into your pricing as well.

Let's say you are worth $50/hour. This means that a 1-hour photo session will cost the client $200.

Invest in a website that stands out

Once you have decided on a name for your photography business, you will need to spend the time and money to create a killer website. There are free sites and templates out there, but your best bet is to pay for a website.

Keep your site organized and break up your photos into galleries. Talk about yourself as the photographer/videographer and your business, as well as what you specialize in.

How to Attract Photography/Videography Clientele

Now that your business is in place, it is time to attract customers to shoot. (Not literally!)

Create your brand

You must set yourself apart from the enormous crowd of other photographers. This means you cannot be everything to everyone. Otherwise, you will fail. Decide what your specialty is, such as couples that want unique wedding photos, for instance. Figure out what makes your business unique and use that to help brand your business.

Network

You will need to network *a lot* as a new photographer. You may be the best in the region, but if people don't know anything about you, then you will never attract business. Ensure people know about you and what your business offers.

Use social media

Social media is one of the best ways to promote photography and videography businesses. I suggest to pick one to two platforms and promote on those consistently. Facebook is a great option, but I would also choose more visual media such as Instagram to showcase your photos and videos.

Growing Your Photography/Videography Business

Now that you got wheels in motion and have attracted some potential clients, you need to keep up the pace!

- **Spice up marketing** by investing in other marketing strategies whenever you can.

- **Use Google Ads** to purchase keywords and generate more traffic to your website.

- **Join charities** that run silent auctions. This helps you get your name in front of people with money to spend, and they can purchase prints from you as well.

- **Create an email list** so that you can contact your fans consistently with news, updates, and promotions.

- **Maintain your blog** and website to help you establish authority in the photography and videography niche.

E-COMMERCE STORE

With the continuous dramatic growth of the internet, it is no surprise that e-Commerce stores are making a combat. With low startup costs and the ease to become visible to search engines, this type of store is a choice many work from home entrepreneurs are choosing.

What is e-Commerce?

Also known as e-Business, these stores are the sale and purchase of goods and services through an electronic medium, a.k.a. the internet. It electronically transfers data and funds between two or more parties. It is better known as online shopping.

Starting your own e-Commerce store is hard work with a ladder of steps that have to come together at the right time to be successful. However, don't let this intimidate you!

Pick a product

The first thing you must do to build an e-Commerce business is to know what kind of products you want to sell and in what niche. This is one of the more challenging areas of starting any online business. Here are some ideas to help you determine what products you want to sell online:

- Look at what you already have
- Locally
- Online trends
- Social curation websites
- Social forums
- Social media
- Competitors
- SEO insights

Assess your idea

When you have a product in mind, how do you know it will be a winning idea?

- Analyze the competition
- Understand your market
- Survey your target market
- Create a campaign to gain funds
- Open a test store

Obtain your product

After you have evaluated your product idea, you need to figure out where you will obtain them:

- Domestic or overseas suppliers
- Look into:
    - Directories
    - Google
    - Local library
- What is the minimum requesting quote, etc.?

Preparation and Research

Research the competition

- Competitive analysis
    - Tools:
        - SimilarWeb
        - Mailcharts
        - Buzzsumo
        - Alexa
        - Facebook Audience Insights
    - Subscribe to their website/blog
    - Follow on social media
    - Purchase their product

Create a business plan

Business plans, as we have talked about before, are the roadmap to your business and help bring your ideas into the light and allow your ideas to come together.

Register your business

There are many options when it comes to registering an online business. Just Google it, and you will find tons of places to look!

Setting Up Your e-Commerce Store

Name your business

Solidifying a business name is another challenging task, as well as deciding on a good and available domain name for your website URL. '*[What Should I Name My Online Store?](#)*' is a great article to start out with!

Develop a logo

Now that you have your business name and a registered domain, you will need to craft a logo yourself or find someone who can. My favorite place is Fiverr, where you can find unique logo designers on a budget!

Grasping Search Engine Optimization (SEO)

Before you jump into the building process of your e-Commerce store, you need to understand the basics of SEO so that you are capable of optimizing your site so that Google ranks it towards the top of search results, thus, attracting more consumers to your online business.

Build your store

There are many vital elements to creating your online store. From writing valuable content to creating descriptions for products and shooting photos that will capture the eye of potential customers, there are many tools that can simplify and speed up this process:

- Resources to create DIY photography
- Product descriptions that sell

Prepare for Launch

There are many essential elements that help to bring your online store all together which you need to prepare:

- Choose a shipping strategy
- Choose shipping and fulfillment strategies
- Define your key performance indicators
- Add store grader to your storefront

Launch Your e-Business!

Your first paying consumer

The hard work begins after you launch. However, there are many ways to learn how to make your very first sale!

Marketing

With some sells under your belt, you need to get serious about your marketing strategy:

- [Craft good welcome emails](#)
- [Create 'abandoned cart' emails as reminders](#)
- [Segment your mailing list for engagement](#)
- [Build an email list that further drives traffic](#)

Drive traffic

- Create and maintain a blog
- Build your audience with video marketing
- Build a following on Instagram and Facebook
- Use different techniques to [drive traffic to your online storefront](#)

James Willner

PATIENT ADVOCATE

If you have an inner desire to help people live the healthiest lives possible but don't want to spend a decade in school or wear scrubs, then starting a patient advocacy business is the next best thing!

If you:

- Are a self-starter
- Have a knack for networking
- Thrive on challenges
- Adapt to change easily
- Are a great listener
- Are self-disciplined
- Can be easily trusted
- Learn from your mistakes
- Like to support those in your everyday life

Then you have what it takes to be a health advisor to patients of all ages, shapes, and sizes.

Your Advocacy Services

There is a wide range of advocate services, such as but not limited to:

- Facilitating communications between medical staff and patients
- Helping with insurance and medical billing
- Assisting patients in their homes

Connect with people you believe could greatly benefit from your services. Listen to what they have to say about your idea, what they need, and what they are willing to pay for your services.

Then, you can make a list of services you feel you are capable of providing that you can start to offer to those in your inner circle that are in need of what you have to offer. To determine the price of your services, it is a good idea to ask questions in your network, as well as to business advisors.

Your Patient Advocacy Clients

Who is going to hire you for these kinds of services? Who will pay you sufficiently to be an advocate for patients in need? This will be your target market. While many people's mind turns right towards older people on Medicare, there is a large market for advocates for the younger population, especially for children who do not have as big of a voice when it comes to medical care.

You will need to brainstorm a list of possibilities of those that may hire you for your advocacy skills:

- Plan to offer medical liaison services? Your target market would be individuals, family members, or insurers of employers

- Plan to offer insurance and billing reconciliation? Then you want to contact referrers who hear from clients who have issues with billing

THE NEW BUSINESS IDEAS

It is also a good idea to plan how you will outreach to your market.

- Make a brochure?
- Develop a website?
- Include or not to include pricing?

Privacy laws

To be a prosperous patient advocate, you will need to understand the HIPAA Laws and instill trust in those that are taking you up on your services as their health care proxy. With each client you work for, you will come across successes. These successes will share their experiences with you to their friends and families, which will build your client base by word of mouth.

James Willner

FREELANCE CONTENT CREATOR

When it comes to the online world, *content is king*. If you are naturally great with words and creating captivating content, then perhaps a freelance writing business is a great place to start in building financial freedom from home.

Being a freelance writer can be overwhelmingly confusing. There are tons of options and no 'traditional' path to follow, which means you are left to figure all that out yourself.

From personal experience, here are the simplest set of steps that I have found to get that freelance content creator business going, starting as soon as *today*. Think about how great it would be to see your name on renowned websites?!

Get a free WordPress blog and post a short article

Starting a blog in 2018 is so simple that your grandparents can do it. It's also the easiest step you can take to get an inch closer to earning a significant income with freelance writing.

You don't even have to pay for WordPress at this point, open an account with the free version and write a blog post about something you care about! A simple 300 to 500-word post will do to get you started. Don't allow yourself to get caught up in that negative self-talk that tries to perfect your post. You don't need the perfect post or perfect website to get started. That all will come later! Just *begin*!

Come up with 3 ideas for niches you would like to write about

One of the most difficult challenges is knowing what kinds of freelance writing jobs to apply for. Freelancing websites are loaded with hundreds of thousands of posts, which can make anyone feel overwhelmed. When there are so many options, you tend to not take any.

This is where choosing niches will come in handy. It filters the jobs that don't apply to you and helps you to focus on standing out with the ones that do. Here is the best way to quickly discover your niche(s):

- Give yourself an hour to think about where and how you spend your time and money. What do you invest many hours in and what do you spend a consistent amount of money on?

- With the time you have remaining, send a message to your friends and family asking what areas you have come up with that you stand out the most. This will show you niches from a 'relative expert' point of view, which means you are the expert and those you ask are beginners.

- Write down the 3 niche ideas you have come up with and use them as a guide to help you filter through the hundreds of freelancing jobs

Pick 5 blogs that pay for posts and bookmark them

There are literally thousands of websites that pay for guest posts and submissions. This will also help you to determine if these are the niches that you like, these are going to be profitable, and if you will be able to work on for a long time.

This is an easy step since there are websites such as *The Write Life* that posts articles with lists of publications on a regular basis. The more solid the opportunities are, the better your portfolio will look in the long run.

Locate 5 freelance job board listings you can see yourself writing

Job boards are a great starting place to get a feel for the freelance job market. You are able to see the businesses that are seeking freelancers and see what is available for you.

Here is a list of some of the best job boards for freelancers. Start here and pick 5 listings that you can see yourself creating. Place them in a spreadsheet or simply bookmark them.

Find a local business directory and determine 5 potential clients

You can simply Google your local area with the phrase 'business directory' to find a thorough database of businesses near you. For instance: *Kansas City, KS + Business Directory.*

You can then look through the list and search for businesses that you think you would like to work with. They can be in your chosen niches or ones that stand out with professional websites and content marketing systems in place.

Email a local business

Once you find a few local businesses that catch your eye, hop over to their website if they have one (most do) and send them a quick email asking if they would be interested in hiring you as a freelance writer to help them curate content for their website.

This can be done even if a business doesn't have a website, as long as you have prices and your portfolio in place. You are simply getting a feel for the opportunities that are out there for you.

I suggest doing this procedure at least once per day because you will have a better chance of landing your first client in a matter of weeks!

Post to Facebook

Your list of Facebook friends is a great source for potential clients when you are just starting out as a freelance writer. It could be someone you know or someone they know. Finding connections is *key*.

My very first two clients were local and were friends of my cousin who she connected me with by simply posting on Facebook and asking! You don't need to make a fancy post, you just go up and shamelessly ask and see if you get any hits in return.

Even if you don't hear anything for a while, you have still managed to reach out to your local community that you have a freelance business. This is a good start in getting the motivation to keep the business rolling and the wheels continuously turning!

Design your business logo

Logos are powerful ways to turn your business from an idea into a reality, which makes it a great place to start in order to take your freelance business seriously!

If you are not great at graphic design, head over to Fiverr and pay a couple bucks to have a logo created for you! Once you like the final design, add it to your email signature to give your emails to clients a professional appeal.

If you are decent at design, I suggest using websites like Canva, which have tons of templates to start out with! It is easy to create a logo there, trust me.

A word from the experienced freelancer:
The key when starting out as a freelance writer newbie is to break the process into tiny chunks, which helps the process become much more manageable. What was a daunting task at first glance can easily be done in five to one-hour exercise.

James Willner

WEBSITE BUYER AND FLIPPER

A popular way to make an easy income from the internet is to buy a product at a lower price and sell it at a higher price. No, we aren't talking about retail arbitrage, but domain flipping!

Domain flipping is simply purchasing domain names that are already registered, flipping them, and selling them for profit. If you don't like the idea of dealing with physical products, this is a great business model for you!

Domain flipping is similar to house flipping but with internet properties instead of real estate properties. Domains aren't the only things you can flip for cash, either. You can also flip completed websites for cash!

THE NEW BUSINESS IDEAS

Domain and Website Flipping 101

What is vital to understand with this business is that even though you purchase a domain or website at a low price, this doesn't necessarily mean you will sell it. Buying and selling domains are comparable to playing in the stock market; you must be aware of the market around you as well as the trends that can impact supply and demand.

There are two main strategies to flip domains:
1. Locate domains that you can sell at a very increased price and profit at least several thousand dollars
2. Sell a large amount of domains on a consistent basis (BEST STRATEGY)

Buying your domain portfolio

The best strategy is to begin by purchasing a large number of domains. For instance, you may spend $1,000 but buy 100 domains. The money you will make this way is locating the domains that people are looking for.

Here are the best places to search for highly desired domains:
- Quality expired domains
- Domain buy and sell sites
- Domain backorder sites
- Expired domain auctions
- Deleted domain sites
- Scraping domains with software

After you have found domains you wish to buy, you then need to register them. I suggest using NameSilo.

Holding domains

Owning domains is not a process that is passive. You will have to park those that have traffic and sell that traffic to make some profit. You can also build websites to some domains that are within profitable niches. Adding links and utilizing affiliate programs can help monetize these sites.

At this point, you may find that there are some domains you wish to keep and others you want to sell for a higher profit margin.

Selling domains

Flipping domains is an active method that requires your time and energy. You cannot purchase a bunch of domains, list them, and watch the money come in.

"Flipping" means you have to do some work to get the domains to a profitable state where people want to buy them from you. It also involves strategic buying and selling in order to make a profit from your efforts.

Best websites to sell domains and websites

- Flippa
- Sedo
- Brand Bucket
- Afternic
- GoDaddy

Don't just get stuck with domains

Most of the time you are able to sell your domain at a much larger price if you take the time to build a website along with it. This is beneficial since it shows the domain's potential, enhances the value of SEO and makes them much more appealing to buyers.

THE NEW BUSINESS IDEAS

GRAPHIC DESIGNER

Do you have an eye for design? Are you motivated enough to earn an additional income by using your skills?

Evaluate your skills

What can and can't you do in graphic design? Many graphic designers are expected to be able to produce:

- Logos
- Business cards
- Website design
- Social media design
- Animation design
- Stationary
- Print design
- Typography design
- Packaging
- Print

- Restaurant
- Infographics

Check the competition

Research the graphic design competition in your geographical area, especially those that are competing with your clientele.

Establish a price list

Will you choose to charge an hourly rate or be paid on a project by project basis? Also, remember that you will have both regular clients and temporary clients.

Be legal

Create a contract that you have your potential clients fill out that captures the following information:

- Requested service
- Delivery schedule

- Estimated cost
- Agreement from both parties
- What must be supplied by client
- Transfer of rights to completed materials
- Limitation of liability
- Cancellation policy

Outsource skills

Thanks to the internet, it is now easier than ever to simply outsource pieces of larger projects to enhance your skills and ensure that clients are satisfied.

Brand yourself

Since you are a graphic designer, you naturally must brand yourself in order to attract clients who will want to work with you. Clients will automatically judge your abilities from what they see from the way you personally brand yourself.

Network

As a graphic designer, just like many other similar jobs, you need to be spending as much time as you can in growing your network with your competition as well as potential clientele. You should be able to comfortably share your business problems and benefit from the experience of those in your same field.

ONLINE DATING CONSULTANT

Advancements to the internet mean that there is an ever-growing market for those in the online dating realm. Online dating consultants are those that help people navigate the online dating world.

Contrary to popular beliefs, many of these websites are not just used to find a spouse. Your job as a consultant in this niche is to fill an array of needs, serious to casual. You are to create unions and make relationships stronger. You play a hand in creating a better community!

The day in the life of an online dating consultant:

- Meetings with clients
- Writing and editing dating profiles
- Crafting responses to messages
- Taking profile photos

- Advertising
- Social media strategies

How you make money

In this work from home business, you will typically charge clients for your time. You should create a package rate that includes different levels of service for designated amounts of time.

If you have a knack for matching people and getting folks to connect with one another, then your potential for business growth can be substantial.

Skills needed:

- Understand what people want
- Don't judge others
- Friendly and personable
- Able to plan ahead accordingly
- Organized
- Able to multitask

THE NEW BUSINESS IDEAS

Costs to begin

Starting an online dating consulting business is cheap to start. You really won't need too many other office supplies besides your computer! I suggest you create a website that advertises and showcases the services you provide, which is where the investment will take place. Plan to spend $150 for a website, advertising, etc.

Steps to start your consultant business:

1. Create a business plan
2. Establish a legal business entity
3. Register for taxes
4. Open a bank account dedicated to business expenses
5. Set up accounting
6. Obtain the required licenses
7. Obtain business insurance
8. Define your brand to stand out
9. Establish a strong web presence

AFFILIATE MARKETER

One of the most efficient and easiest ways to make money online is by creating your own affiliate marketing business or adding affiliate marketing to your existing business model.

What is affiliate marketing?

Affiliate marketing allows you to make money online without a website or your own product by advertising and promoting other people's products and services and then receiving a commission in return.

Steps to Launch Affiliate Marketing Business

Choose an affiliate network

You will need to find a right fit between you and the business that is going to benefit from your promotional efforts. There are hundreds of affiliate networks out there, with some of the most popular being Amazon, Apple, Google, and Clickbank.

There are also individual entrepreneurs who have created awesome products that are worth a look as well. Many companies online have their own affiliate program that you can apply to in order to promote their products and/or services.

Research and pick affiliate products

As a new affiliate marketer, you need a sound product strategy. You need to choose a niche that has many vendors to choose from. Limit yourself to 2 to 3 products at a time, so that you can learn and become more of an expert that others can trust online.

The more comfortable you become an affiliate marketer, the more you can dive into specialized and broad niches.

Think about buying the product before promoting

You are never obligated to purchase things from companies before promoting them, but when you own and have used something, this helps you to establish credibility and trust in the niche you are in. Plus, you will have intimate knowledge of that product which can mean a big difference between landing sales and missing out on customers.

I have found that creating product reviews is a superb way to enhance your overall credibility as an affiliate marketer, no matter the niche you are in. Share case studies and your personal experiences with products.

Use social media to get more traffic

There are tons of free traffic sources out there to get more people in front of your affiliate links:

THE NEW BUSINESS IDEAS

- YouTube
- Pinterest
- Instagram
- Twitter
- Facebook
- Snapchat

And many others! Video marketing is the most popular and works best since it is more than capable of demonstrating a product, rather than reading your commentary and seeing pictures.

James Willner

SOCIAL MEDIA MANAGER

Social media used to be just a fun way to connect with those you love. Now, it has grown into an affordable way to market businesses of all shapes and sizes. Many businesses, however, get overwhelmed by all the tasks associated with managing multiple social media platforms, which is where you can take advantage as an entrepreneur!

What is a social media manager?

As a social media manager, you offer services that your clients need, such as but not limited to:

- Staying current with trends
- Posting graphics and content
- Setting up accounts
- Developing market strategies based on your client's goals
- Increasing the number of followers
- Customer service

- Marketing analysis
- Community facilitation

What does it take to become a social media manager?

- Understands social media and how it can be used as a marketing tool
- Has knowledge of nuances on various platforms
- Has the ability to develop strategies to meet the client's goals and objectives
- Captures the client's voice with graphics and well-written content
- Manages several media platforms for a large number of clients

Steps to starting a social media manager business:

Build your own following on social media

Before you try to land clients that need your services, you should work on building your very own social media influence on a variety of platforms. This means more than just a large number of followers, you need to build a following that engages with you.

Study social media

Platforms are ever-changing, which means marketing evolves as well, requiring you to stay up-to-date on the changes and trends.

Decide what type of services you want to offer

You can decide to either offer an array of package deals or a full-service package that includes everything from creating the account(s), creating and posting content and moderating commentary from the community.

Develop your business plan

This plan doesn't have to be too complex, just ensure you have a strategic roadmap that will help you build upon your initial success.

- Goals
- Services
- Liabilities and assets
- Marketing
- Competition

Decide on pricing

Social media managers earn anywhere from $48,000 to $75,000 yearly. If you are starting a brand-new business, it can take a while to see this amount. Testimonials and referrals are a must in helping you earn bigger bucks.

Obtain licensing

You can get the correct licenses or permits by contacting your city or county about business licenses.

Continue to work on your plan

Once everything is in place, you must keep the momentum up to continue getting and keeping clients. Networking is essential in this business and will be the best strategy to grab initial clients.

THE NEW BUSINESS IDEAS

BLOGGING

While blogging for many businesses is a tool to continue success, many other people just like you started blogging and have managed to turn this into their full-time careers.

Businesses of all shapes and sizes have a challenge of building their audience who sees and purchases their products. Blogger works backward, building an audience and then putting out great content that consumers want to come back to.

What is a blog?

A blog is a web page that is meant for regularly posted content. Blogs are meant to take on a personal tone compared to articles and publications, so bloggers are able to connect on a deeper level with their audience. People start blogs for a variety of reasons, such as:

- Selling products and/or services
- Building their personal brand and obtaining authority
- Building email lists
- Teaching others
- Sharing experiences, opinions, passions, etc.

STEPS TO STARTING A BLOG

Pick a niche

While it may seem hard to stand out among the thousands of other bloggers and their contents, you can be assured that things have not been talked about or explained in *your* words yet. You can compete with others by picking a specific audience while creating content that is not easily found anywhere else online.

- Focus on one location
- Focus on segments of a larger category
- Deliver content in your style of voice

- Compete with quality

Choose your platform

This is typically where many beginning bloggers get stuck and quit. You will have to choose between self-hosted or hosted platforms. There are also free-hosted platforms, such as Tumblr. I suggest a hosted platform for beginners, WordPress.com being my number one recommendation!

Choose a name and a blog theme

Shopping for a domain name for your blog is a great time to brainstorm what your website will be called. I highly suggest not using your name unless you are planning on building your personal brand.

Once you settle on a name, you get to pick a blog theme. Depending on the platform you chose, there are plenty of beautiful free themes to choose from to get started. Once you know how your platform works, have developed content, and are getting traffic to your blog, then you may consider a paid theme to spice things up.

Lay the groundwork

Distribution is what so many bloggers struggle with. This is because they fail to have a concrete strategy within their process of publishing. Plus, publishing is already a nervous experience enough, then they amplify this, making it scarier than it really is.

- Start collecting emails ASAP
- Search for the opportunity to go after search engine traffic by optimizing SEO
- Set up a solid social media strategy
- Reduce, reuse, resurface old content
- Understand the analytics of your core audience
- Plan out your publishing strategy

Blogging is one of those businesses that can take up an entire book by itself, if not multiple ones. I suggest you research online about blogging, watch YouTube tutorials, and play around with free blogging websites such as Weebly.com or Wix.com. There is also a free version of WordPress, WordPress.org.

James Willner

CHATBOT CREATOR

You know when you are unsatisfied with a product, but you don't want to talk on the phone or email customer service? I am sure you try to search for a chat box that you can speak with a representative over internet chat.

Chatbots are not a new thing, but they have become a hot topic in technology and digital marketing. Many of us have interacted with one at some point, either as an automated telephone assistant or a modernized chatbot online.

Artificial intelligence (AI) has been used for a few years now to carry out tasks and give out information with no human beings being involved. If you are a technology guru and stay up on the trends, then creating a chatbot agency might be worth considering.

Becoming the boss of a chatbot agency is not the easiest work from home job, especially since these bots are still in early development. However, if you dip your toes into this now, you are bound to make bunches of money from this opportunity.

Steps to Chatbot Agency Creation

Select a platform

There are many platform options out there that offer an array of varying benefits and features. Some bot builders will require you to have various levels of knowledge. If you have coding expertise, then you will have an easier time.

Analyze bot's audience

You will have to touch base with clients you are working for who want a chatbot created so that you can successfully target their key audience. Different bots are created to give information or solve issues, or work as a type of sales funnel.

Market your chatbots

Consider what your bot's marketability is during the creation process. You should come up with a unique, attractive name that is easy to remember. Ensure that you are easily available on social media platforms and other chatbot databases. This will make your company's bot easy to locate.

Enhance

Chatbots, like other modern tools, are dynamic solutions that can continuously be optimized to perform even better. Once you have a bot that has been running for a bit, look at its performance and make changes.

THE NEW BUSINESS IDEAS

CRAFT BREWERY

Instead of just going out to taste and enjoy ales with friends, have you ever wondered what it would be like to make your own cold brews? If you have, perhaps starting a craft brewery is for you!

While it may sound fun, there's a lot that goes into the planning, money, and patience of starting a craft brewery from scratch.

Equipment

How much your equipment costs vary on the size of your brewery and whether you purchase things new or used.

- Smallest capacity brewing equipment
    - 1 barrel – 31 gallons of beer = $100,000 or less
- Larger capacity
    - 30-barrel system = 1 million dollars

Your brewery will need these essentials:

- Kettles
- Kegs
- Boilers
- Bottling and canning lines
- Conveyors
- Cooling system
- Storage tanks
- Fermentation tanks
- Filters
- Beer-labelers
- Piping and tubing
- Cleaning supplies
- Waste treatment system
- Tap handles

Location

Picking an ideal location is essential to your brewery's success. If you have an already established building, great! You will just have to pay for renovations. Most times, however, it may be a better and easier idea to construct from scratch.

Other costs

One of the biggest things for breweries that is often overlooked is the composite flooring. This type of floor can better withstand shock, temperature differences, and acid from beer.

There are also license requirements that you will need to adhere too. You will have to apply for a federal brewing permit, which can take 4 or more months to process through the Alcohol and Tobacco Tax Trade Bureau. To get approved for a permit, you must have all of your equipment installed and in operation.

James Willner

CRAFTER

If you are a creative person that is looking for a low-cost business idea to start from home, there are many ways you can let your rainbow of creativity shine from art to crafts and much more.

Create something that people will *want* to buy

The reality of the crafting world is that you will need to transition from things you like to make to relax to items that people will want to purchase from you.

- Is there a market for what you are crafting?
- Are people willing to pay what you need to make a profit?

Work on your items every day

Remember that your business is a marathon, not a sprint. No matter how low sales are or frustrated you become, as an entrepreneur, it is important to not stop and keep up the momentum. Dedication and patience are two key factors that you need!

Be professional but friendly

Handmade businesses rely heavily on you being friendly with both your established and potential consumers. They are buying from you because they want something unique.

This means that you need to:
- Make it easy for them to get into contact with you
- Take good photos of products you are selling
- Be good at telling your homemade business story
- And remember that your consumers are not your buddies
    - Respond to inquiries in detail promptly
    - Use salutations when writing

- Don't get angry with people that make unreasonable demands
- Don't complain about other consumers in customers forums

Take gorgeous photos

In all businesses that are based online, this is crucial. The more eye-catching your photos, the more consumers will be attracted to buy what you have to sell.

- Filtered white light or naturally lit
- Consistent
- Simple
- Iconic backgrounds
- Clear and crisp shots
- Interesting angles

Create items that are reproducible

The truth is, you are only going to be able to scale your handmade business so much by making one-of-a-kind items when selling online.

Once your business begins to take off, you will find that taking photos, writing titles and descriptions for all new items will eat into your time to manage your business.

Believe in yourself and be adaptable

If you fail to believe in yourself and your skills, you will never succeed. It takes dedication and time to make a living selling your handmade goods online. If you are making something you don't love, then you will eventually run out of steam and give up on your business. In other words, love what you are doing *fiercely*.

You will also need to be adaptable to changes. If you are working day and night and your business is still not scaling upwards, something needs to change. Love what you are doing but be open to changes that are required for your business to succeed.

Develop a mailing list

You can blog and utilize social media platforms all day every day and still never receive the number of consumers you can attract with email marketing. Mailing lists are the best ways to prospect new people for making sales.

Price for profit

This is one of the biggest problems you see in the handmade communities. Many people start off selling their work from the perspective of a hobbyist. They don't really know what the price for their items should be, which means they underprice things.

There will almost always be a competitor selling something similar to you. Do not attempt to compete with price! Do the work to figure out what you need to sell your items at. If you are serious about making a living from handmade items, this is a must.

Create a website or blog

When you are selling online, you need to invest in a domain name so that it is easy to transfer consumers to your online store. As soon as you can have your own self-hosted website, the better. You should also begin blogging on the side as well. This is a great way to truly craft your business's story and the work you do.

Startup Ideas for Creative Entrepreneurs

- Art academy
- Bridal store
- Costume jewelry
- Crochet knitting
- Custom mobile cover printing
- Decorative candle making
- Designed bed sheet maker
- Designed bindi making
- Decorative lace making
- Designer saree making

- Designer jute bag maker
- Embroidery garments maker
- Greeting card creator
- Interior designer
- Kid garments
- Logo design
- Makeup artist
- Online t-shirts
- Necktie maker
- Papad maker
- Picker maker
- Rakhi maker
- Soft toys maker
- Wedding gift packager
- Woodworking

Places to Sell Your Creations and Creative Services

- Artfire
- Bonanza
- Craftsy

THE NEW BUSINESS IDEAS

- Dawanda
- eBay
- eCrater
- Etsy
- Folksy
- GLC Craft Mall
- Handmade Artists' Shop
- Handmade at Amazon
- Hyena Cart
- iCraft
- Made It Myself
- Meylah
- Misi
- Shop Handmade
- Society6
- SpoonFlower
- Zibbit

James Willner

TOUR GUIDE

If you love showing your friends new and unseen places in your very own city, have you ever considered being a tour guide for others and getting *paid for it*?

Evaluate your city

- Is your city a popular destination for tourists?
- What is trending?
- Anything cool to explore?

Check in with your city's tourism board to see if they have the information to help you outline possible opportunities.

Identify your market

- What kind of people would be attracted to a tour in your city?
- Are they the outdoorsy type?
- Do they enjoy new food?

- Will they want to speak with locals?
- What gets them excited?

Determining your target customers will help you make a lot of essential decisions.

Register your business

Head over to your local tourism board to ensure you meet the requirements to start a tourist company in your city/area.

Other logistics:

- Name your business
- Register it
- Get licenses and permits
- Open a separate bank account
- Get liability insurance

Design a tour

- Create your business plan
- Create your selling proposition

- Determine your price
- Craft a story
- Create a logo
- Build a website
- Signup with online booking websites

Build relationships

- Speak with other tour guides
- Spend time with a mentor
- Become active in your community
- Attend seminars

Market your tours

- List your tour(s) on online travel agents
- Implement good SEO practices
- Buy AdWords
- Start email marketing
- Advertise on social media
    - Post on Facebook
    - Add photos to Instagram
- Use analytics to know what is and isn't working

Launch your tour!

Host friends and family members first as a test run. This helps you to collect as much feedback as you can and help you to feel confident in your guiding abilities.

James Willner

REPAIR SERVICES

There are many kinds of repair business opportunities if you have a knack for fixing things that people are trying to find a cheaper way to fix!

Starting a home-based repair business is a great way to learn as you get your feet wet in the land of entrepreneurs. Repair services are easy to start and have a low-cost entry to get started. This business type if typically profitable without the risk of other businesses.

Are you cut out for this type of business?

Your wisdom and your planning skills will not determine your success in any home repair business. Instead, your motivation is what will be the determining factor of a success or a failing business. If you have the ability to get things done in a reasonable allotment of time, then you are bound to see profits as a result.

Remember that you are your own boss; there is no one to give you a boost of motivation and keep you accountable for your actions.

What services do you plan to offer?

List out skills you are good at and then decide which one of those you would enjoy the most doing. What services get you excited? People usually enjoy what they are good at the most. If you are good at repairing washing machines, for instance, you can make huge profits from it since most folks despise this.

Obtain proper licensing

Licensing is required for particular trades and each state has varying laws in regard to licenses and permits. Ensure to check into your state laws before you start advertising your home repair services.

What homes will you repair?

It is best to choose a specific niche of customers you will repair for and advertise to. There are two main factors in determining your target audience"

- What consumer base needs your repair services the most
- Who is the most willing to pay for it?

Another thing to consider is the type of people you want to work with. If you like your customers, your business will be much more enjoyable.

Setting up shop

- Choose a name for your business
- Choose a business structure for your handyman business
- Open a separate bank account
- Have a logo designed
- Create business cards

- Set up a separate business address
- Get liability insurance

Market your business

During the first few months of starting your business from scratch, marketing is where you will spend a lot of time. Being awesome and well-branded won't have customers pouring in automatically.

One of the quickest ways to gain customers in this genre of home-based business is by posting ads on Craigslist.com. Online marketing will give you many more leads than other old-school methods such as newspaper ads and flyers. It is also much more cost effective.

Repair Business Ideas

- Car dent repair
- Body shop
- Commercial oven cleaning
- Factory cleaning
- Headlight cleaning
- Curb painting
- Car painting
- Car wrapping
- Home-based credit repair
- Computer repair
- Shoe repair
- Toilet repair
- Fireplace repair
- Wheel repair
- Bleacher repair
- Blind installation and cleaning
- Collision repair
- Video game console repair
- Windshield repair
- Rock chip repair

THE NEW BUSINESS IDEAS

- Coffee equipment repair
- BBQ grill repair
- Basement repair and restoration
- Cell phone repair
- Vinyl repair
- Leather repair
- Dental repair
- Golf cart repair
- Railcar repair
- Umbrella repair
- Typewriter repair
- GPS repair
- Air conditioning and heating repair
- Awning and canopy repair, installation, cleaning
- Boat repair
- Aircraft engine repair
- Asphalt repair and maintenance
- Gas pump repair
- Locked out of car service
- Server repair
- Washing machine and dryer repair

- Upholstery repair
- Bumper repair
- Car radio repair
- Gun repair
- Appliance repair
- Lift and escalator repair
- DVD repair
- Radiator repair
- Doll repair
- Camera repair
- Water heater repair
- Music repair
- Transmission repair
- Printer repair
- Ice maker repair
- Grain equipment repair
- Refrigerator repair
- Water pump repair
- Tire repair
- Motorcycle repair
- iPod repair

CONCLUSION

Congrats! You have now absorbed the information of 21 different business ideas that are easy to start and develop to earn an extra or full-time income as soon as *today*!

If you have doubts that you can start your own business from home or on-the-go, you are not alone. There are many folks out there that have never taken the leap to take back the reigns on their financial freedom because they feel they are not 'experts' or knowledgeable enough in a field to begin a business of their own.

Get rid of this mindset by knowing that, yes, you are not an expert, but you can *become* one! With the endless territory of the internet, there are plenty of resources to learn more about the business you want to create. It is up to *you* to take that first step.

I hope that this book was informative and able to provide you with all the tools you need to achieve your goals of financial freedom as you break the chains of the average 9 to 5 job!

The next step is to pick a business model that you enjoyed reading about. What business type caught your eye the most? If there is more than one, then write them out and research more about them. Get creative! There is no rule-book saying you can't combine ideas as well! You are the only one placing limits on yourself.

Finally, if you found this book useful in anyway, a review on Amazon is always appreciated!

www.ingramcontent.com/pod-product-compliance
Lightning Source LLC
Chambersburg PA
CBHW071558220526
45469CB00003B/1055